You Can Control Your Class

ORDER DIRECTLY FROM
ANN ARBOR PUBLISHERS LTD.
P.O. BOX 1, BELFORD
NORTHUMBERLAND NE70 7JX
TEL. 01668 214460 FAX 01668 214484
www.annarbor.co.uk

Cover Design & Interior Illustrations: Nanette M. Brichetto

Academic Therapy Publications
20 Commercial Boulevard
Novato, California 94949-6191

Tests, books, and materials for and about the learning disabled

International Standard Book Number: 1-57128-017-0

9 8 7 6 5 4 3
3 2 1 0 9 8 7 6 5

Table of Contents

Foreword

Various surveys, including the annual Gallup poll on education, indicate that discipline, or rather a lack of it, is the biggest problem in education today.

For the past several decades, a sizable portion of our youth have been on a "freedom kick," which boils down to their not wanting anyone, especially any parent, teacher or adult, to tell them what to do. We can't blame them too much for this attitude since it is human nature for the young to want to assert their rights and grow in a topsy-turvy way. The fault lies not with them, but with us, their important adults, for not teaching them positive discipline at an early age.

We're raising a generation of "TV addicts" who are often deprived of the enriching experiences of home and family responsibilities. The pendulum has swung much too far in the direction of "freedom" and self-indulgence. If the situation is not righted, we won't have any freedoms left worth shouting about. We must find a better balance between freedom and discipline.

The thesis of this book is that discipline must be taught and mastered thoroughly. Mere exposure is not sufficient. Discipline is the very foundation upon which all success rests, including academic success.

The ultimate goal is to teach the student the ability to know how to act appropriately in diverse settings where there may be no set rules. This calls for a highly trained and disciplined mind more than an obeisant spirit and body. Each student must be taught to think for himself and act in socially responsible ways.

We have all seen teachers who were strict and the students complied while in the teacher's presence, but when a substitute came into the classroom, it was chaos. In these instances, the lessons of discipline were not learned to the point of internalization.

The real challenge is to provide the type of discipline that will motivate students to behave appropriately in all situations, developing inner controls rather than relying on external pressures; however, *we have to learn to walk before we can learn to run*. We have to begin with the external pressures *(imposed discipline)* and then gradually and skillfully move to develop the inner controls (self-discipline).

This book, which emphasizes the more elementary phases of discipline, is prepared with the conscious realization that teachers can control their students and classes. You *can* plan, initiate and implement desirable changes which will put you in command rather than continue to tolerate deteriorating situations that will eventually make your job intolerable.

Here are two big bonuses for following this program:

1. Your job will become easier and more enjoyable.
2. The learning program in your classroom will be strengthened.

Introduction

This book is written to help teachers gain and maintain better control in the classroom. Although the experience of the authors has been mainly in the elementary school, we feel that the principles and techniques discussed in the book are applicable to all levels of instruction.

There are four major premises underlying the philosophy of this book:

1. The success of any learning program is predicated on successful control.

2. Teacher attitude toward the profession of teaching is directly related to control.

3. Emphasis on classroom management techniques is far more efficient than emphasis on coping with disruptive students.

4. The students have a *right* to learn in an atmosphere conductive to productive learning.

The Learning Program and Control

We feel that effective learning programs and effective control in the classroom are equally important. While effective control without a good learning program is useless, a good learning program without any control invariably dooms the program to failure and often leads to premature abandonment of the program. We also recognize that some learning programs have a built-in control factor. The program may motivate the students so that they are too busy or too interested in the activity to get into mischief – indeed, a very good control technique. However, most programs are based on the assumption that the class is firmly under a teacher's control.

A Positive Attitude Toward Teaching

After years of observing teachers who either think that teaching is "heaven" or that teaching is "hell," the authors feel that the greatest common factor in teacher attitude toward teaching is that of control or lack of it. The teacher who virtually loves teaching is almost always one who has the ability to teach effectively in a class where control is not a problem. On the other hand, a teacher who is in tears at the end of the day and who constantly looks forward to the weekend or summer vacation is in most cases a teacher who has not learned to cope with classroom control; that is, the students will not behave in a manner acceptable to the teacher.

Efficiency and Classroom Management

Furthermore, it is assumed that by following certain time-tested classroom management techniques, the problems with disruptive students will be minimized. This does not mean that if the principles and techniques in this book are followed, there will be no disruptive students in the class. It does mean that if a teacher can apply the principles and techniques in this book so that an atmosphere of mutual trust and respect is established, the vast majority of problems that normally happen in a class will not happen. We firmly believe that it is far easier and more efficient in the long run to spend the time necessary to train and guide students into acceptable behavior than to allow them to become disruptive and then take remedial action.

The Right to Learn

Finally, we feel that a teacher has an obligation to protect the rights of the majority of the students to be able to learn in a classroom relatively free of major distractions. The limits that a teacher should go in accepting disruptive behavior should be measured by the extent to which it is interfering with the rights of others to learn. The teachers should constantly ask this question, "Is it fair to the rest of the class or is it violating the class's rights to learn without distraction?"

CHAPTER I

Time and Effort to Gain Control

Quite often in the rush to start school, teachers feel great pressure to begin the instruction immediately so as not to waste any of the students' time. This obsession with learning efficiency is frequently counter-productive to the total learning experienced by the pupils during a school year. The behavior of the students is neglected in this mad rush toward catching "golden moments" of learning. From our experience we have found that if you take the time to develop a productive learning atmosphere, the total learning will be accelerated, students will have a more positive attitude, and you'll enjoy teaching more.

Accelerated Learning

Simply stated, a teacher who takes the time to get good class control will be able to teach the pupils far more in the long run than one who is continually struggling with disruptive behavior.

We have observed teachers who have felt compelled to rush headlong into the academic part of the curriculum without taking time to get control. Far too often, this neglect of control results in the teachers spending a disproportionate amount of time later "keeping the lid on" and too little time in productive learning. This type of teacher seems to lack the ability to set up behavioral goals and to make a systematic effort to achieve those goals. By the end of the year the net result is confusion, chaos and little solid learning going on in the classroom.

On the other hand, we have observed teachers who have the foresight to look down the road and realize that the class won't learn much unless the students are listening, are capable of following directions, and are sticking to the task until completion. These teachers do take the time necessary at the first of the year to get the class on the path to productive learning. For the most part, these teachers spent minimum time in controlling and maximum time in teaching.

More Positive Student Attitude

In addition to accelerated learning, the initial time invested is also worthwhile in developing feelings of security and self-worth in the pupil. A student who is continually berated, harangued, or is the object of other forms of relatively ineffective control techniques is most likely to develop poor attitudes toward himself. In contrast, the student who is in a classroom where he is taught to be self-directed and allowed to maintain his dignity is bound to have a better feeling about himself and school.

Besides increased self-worth, students feel more secure in situations where rules are made crystal-clear, limits set, and measures taken to enforce them.

Summary

Like anything worthwhile, good classroom control does require time, effort, and commitment on the part of the teacher, especially at the beginning of the year; however, less time and effort will be expended in the long run on non-productive activities. The truth of the matter is that the teacher who has the class under control will be spending more time in solid teaching and liking the job more. Besides, the students will have better feelings about themselves.

CHAPTER II

Letting the Students Know

You can't expect the students to do what you want unless they know exactly what it is you want them to do, and they realize the importance of doing it. We have found great success on holding class meetings for this purpose and then having the students practice for a desired behavior.

Meeting with Our Class

Getting off on the right foot seems to be far easier than correcting unwanted habits and behavior. Therefore, we recommend meetings be held at the earliest possible time. There are certain critical behaviors that will need attention immediately. We recommend that the first class meeting be held on the very first day to tell the class about an important rule or a desired behavior. We personally give first priority to student "self-starting activities" at the beginning of the school year (see Chapter IV). As a result, we spend our first class meeting working on this behavior. As time goes on, we hold other class meetings, but we seldom work on more than one behavior at a time.

The amount of time needed for these meetings will depend on the complexity and importance of the rule or behavior. Generally, they range from 10 to 20 minutes. Certainly, the meetings shouldn't last more than 30 minutes because of the attention span of most of the class.

Although these initial meetings will require quite a bit of time, as the year goes on, less time will be spent dealing with problems such as inappropriate teasing, shoving and pushing in class, etc. These are the problems that seem to crop up during the school year.

The Setting of the Meetings

If you don't want the students to take these meetings lightly, arrange to hold them in a setting that will emphasize their importance. In planning the setting, you should consider not only the time and the place, but other factors such as lighting and student seating arrangements. Everything possible should be done to communicate to the students that this is, indeed, an important time.

If you are in a team-teaching situation, the students should be brought to a central meeting point and a listening atmosphere established. A critical point in establishing the importance of the meeting is to require all the staff of the team to attend the meeting and pay attention to the teacher giving the presentation. Absolutely no conversation is permitted at this time, especially among the teachers.

In a self-contained classroom, gather the students in a special meeting place where you have them close to you in a different setting than you have in your normal classroom instruction. Here again the main emphasis is that the students are listening carefully to what is being discussed. All distractions should be avoided, and precautions need to be taken to make sure students have nothing in their hands at this time.

We have found the following method to be effective in getting students to obey school rules and policies. The method involves four steps:

1. Explanation
2. Demonstration
3. Practicing
4. Retraining

Explaining

The teacher explains the desired behavior. All questions are answered at this time. (In most cases, a simple explanation is not enough. A certain percentage of the students won't listen, a few more will not really understand what you mean, and a few will require more than words for the internalization of the behavior.)

Demonstration

Role-playing, involving both students and teachers, can be an excellent method of conveying the idea. We have had students role-play the wrong way and the right way. An evaluation after each demonstration is useful in making sure every student has a clear understanding of the behavior, its limits, and exceptions.

Practicing

The most important part of the procedure is the involvement of all the students in a practice session. The students are told in advance that those who fail to respond correctly will be given additional training.

Retraining

If a few students are unable to perform adequately during the practice session or fail to internalize the behavior, they are given additional training at recess or after school.

Example

If we wanted students to line up promptly on the playground when the ending recess bell rings, we would first gather the students in a large group and tell them that they are to stop playing and start toward the doors when they hear the bell. Next, we would demonstrate by using a teacher and a student in a role-playing situation. At first, the student does it the wrong way by throwing the ball one more time after the bell rings. Then, after a short evaluation, the role-playing of the correct way is performed.

The students are then taken to the playground and allowed to play for a few seconds. The bell rings and the students stop playing and walk toward the door. The teachers observe during this practice time to see if any student needs further training. Students are observed at different periods to see if one or two are not responding. These students are given training after school.

This procedure can be effective in many areas of classroom control and management such as: bringing instant quiet in the classroom on a given signal or word, discouraging the students from raising their hands when someone is talking to the class, correcting the teacher in a polite way, moving from one place to another in an orderly manner, or beginning work promptly when the bell rings.

CHAPTER III

Three Cardinal Rules

While many different methods are used by various teachers to gain control, there are usually three that are found in classes where good control always prevails. They are:

1. waiting for the student's attention before talking,

2. knowing what your students are doing at all times, and

3. praising in public while reproving in private.

1. Don't talk unless students are listening.

There may be a few exceptional teachers who are so dynamic that anything they do or say will catch the students' attention. However, most of us will be better off if we insist the students are quiet and ready to listen before we start talking. Now this rule may seem rather obvious, but it is amazing how many teachers ignore it. The end result is that very little of what the teacher is saying is listened to by anyone.

First of all, you need some method of initially getting their attention. We use a key phrase, "Please, may I have your attention . . . NOW!" (We use "Practicing" for desired behavior, as described in the previous chapter, to make sure that they do stop and listen.) Almost any signal will work equally well. The main thing is that the students are aware that something the teacher is doing or saying means – quiet.

After you have their attention, you must know what you are going to say. Say it as clearly and concisely as possible. If at any time they stop listening while you are talking you must stop and do whatever is necessary to get them listening again. Here are a few techniques to get them back with you:

1. Stop in the middle of a sentence and wait for eye-to-eye contact.
2. Give positive reinforcement to the ones who are listening by saying something such as, "I do like the way most of you are listening, but there are two or three who could be listening a little better."
3. As a last resort, use the key phrase or signal again. Regardless of how you do it, *you must not go on unless they are all listening.*

2. Know what students are doing.

There is a story, probably apocryphal, about how the sea lion keeps from being eaten by the polar bear. It seems that the polar bear creeps up on the sea lion who sleeps near the water's edge. The sea lion sleeps but a few seconds, then raises its head and looks around for any danger. When the sea lion looks up, the white bear quickly places his black nose into the snow. Now the moral of this story is – the sea lion *who looks up often enough* will be able to slip into the water before the polar bear reaches him and will live to see another day.

Just as the survival of the sea lion depends on his being aware of the surroundings at all times, so does the teacher's survival depend upon his/her being aware of everything that is going on in the classroom. This doesn't mean that you will necessarily have to do something about everything that is going on; you may wish to ignore some of the happenings, but you must be aware of them. Furthermore, it is also important that the students themselves realize that you have knowledge of what they are doing. The best way to insure that you have a good psychological climate in the classroom is by showing that you are genuinely interested in your students' behavior.

Too often, we observe teachers who continually get so involved with a student or a project, they are oblivious to what is happening in the class. Like the sea lion, they cannot do this and easily survive. A pleasant classroom climate can exist only when the class is controlled. (Many teachers who possess all the techniques for good control fail to achieve it because they lack this one important skill of being aware of the actions of their students.) The saddest thing about this situation is that the children know they are not being watched by the teacher and this gives added impetus to their misbehavior. For example: A teacher may notice a student who is in need of help and may get so involved with this one particular student that he/she fails to look up and periodically observe the class. Of course, the class may be doing fine, and the teacher may think that the routine check is unnecessary, but it is courting disaster to make a habit of ignoring your class. Quite frankly, the misbehavior that children may indulge in if they think they would not be noticed, could result in physical injury to one of the students. Teachers do have a responsibility to prevent this. In addition, much misbehavior is an infringement on the right of the rest of the class to learn.

While being aware that everything that is happening at all times is of critical importance, we realize that it is much easier said than done. The habit of looking up at the class must be developed just as you would any good habit. If you are writing at your desk, for instance, write a line or two and then look up. If you are reading, read a paragraph and look up. If you are putting up a bulletin board, put a piece of paper up and then look at the class. How often should one look up? Often enough to be able to say, "I pretty well knew what all the students were doing during that last period or activity."

Continual awareness of class behavior does *not* mean you shouldn't strive to internalize self-control in the class. Indeed, having a class that is self-directed and students who obey rules because they really see a need for obeying them and not from fear of being punished for disobedience is certainly something all teachers should work toward. But until you can be absolutely sure they will behave themselves whether they are observed or not, you must be acutely aware of what they are doing at all times.

3. Praise in public, reprove in private.

Positive reinforcement by use of praise can be very effective in bringing about socially acceptable behavior. If done judiciously, praising in public is about the most effective way of giving the student a reward for desirable behavior, and it costs the teacher nothing. We have found our self-starting activities to be an excellent opportunity to publicly praise our students. However, we try not to overdo it. We try to give them just enough to lead them into the habit of self-starting so they can feel pride in being independent. Certainly they feel no pride in praise that is undeserved. Therefore, the praise should be honest and in proper proportion to the students' efforts and the situation.

Praising in public focuses on the desired behavior of the entire class and further clarifies it. In addition, there are these valuable spinoffs: children not only perceive themselves as being more worthwhile human beings, but surprisingly enough, the teachers also feel better about themselves as a result of smiling and complimenting the students for proper behavior.

On the other hand, reproving in private can pay equally big dividends in guiding the students toward acceptable behavior. First of all, this method allows a child to maintain his dignity. He is free to take a look at what he has done without having to cope with feelings of embarrassment. Also to be considered is the perception the child has of the teacher who is thoughtful enough to spare unneeded embarrassment in front of his peers. To gain the student's respect, the teacher needs to be a model of how to respect others' feelings.

Remember praise pays off, costs nothing, and can be most effective when done publicly, while reproving a child privately costs nothing, yet preserves the child's most valuable possession – his feeling of self-worth.

CHAPTER IV

The Miracle of Self-Starting

Simply stated, self-starting means the students come into the room with a purpose in mind. The students will automatically perform some previously assigned task without direct teacher supervision. If you use self-starting activities, you will have fewer control problems, students will internalize self-direction, teacher and pupil time will be saved, and you will be providing an opportunity for overlearning.

One of the most impressive aspects of self-starting is that once it is established, the students develop the habit of independent work. It becomes virtually impossible for a student to enter the room and not start work. If he doesn't get down to business, he will stick out like a sore thumb. Even the most reluctant student will want to do what the rest of the students are doing. We have had students who have previously refused to do any work, but after a week of self-starting, they were completing all their tasks. The habit had been established. If you once get the students started, you've got a good chance of keeping them going. (Would you believe a 99.4 percent chance?)

Self-starting is self-perpetuating because it gives a child a chance to do an assignment he already knows how to do and thus to start the period with success. The teacher is given an important opportunity to circulate and personally compliment the students on their good habits. In both cases, task success and teacher reinforcement, the child's self-confidence is built.

Self-starting can easily be taught with the use of certain techniques while avoiding some pitfalls. The activities for self-direction can come from almost all areas of the curriculum.

A workable plan for implementing self-starting in the classroom consists of these steps:

1. Explaining the desired behavior to the students
2. Practicing the desired behavior in a hypothetical situation
3. Having the students self-start in a real life situation
4. Maintaining the behavior by positive reinforcement and periodical evaluation

A key to successful self-starting is that the students be assigned only the tasks they can perform without teacher instruction. This means that these self-starting activities cannot be used to learn a new skill or concept. For example, students who had not been previously instructed in writing limericks would not be expected to start the period by writing a limerick. However, a limerick would be entirely appropriate after teacher-directed experience. Also, great care should be taken to make instructions for the activities concise and clear.

Generally speaking, self-starting behavior is quite easily accomplished. However, teachers should be aware of certain pitfalls. One of these is inconsistent effort. Once self-starting has been initiated, the teacher must provide a self-directed activity to start the period every day, and in turn the students must be expected to start on their own *every day*. After a few days without self-starting activities, the students lose the habit of self-starting. On the other hand, while consistency in providing activities should be maintained, repetition of the same activity to the point of boredom should be avoided. After all, limericks every day for a year might be too much.

By observing the class in its self-starting activities, the teachers can identify those few who require further training, thus avoiding badgering the whole class for the lack of performance by a few. Self-starting is not meant to allow the teacher extra time out of the classroom. The teacher's presence is necessary in order for this program to maintain success over a long period of time.

A good example of this procedure was used during the first part of our math period. An explanation was made to the students that there would be a ten-problem quiz written on the board for them to automatically start on when they returned from recess. A practice session was given to the students in which they actually left the room and then returned as if from recess and began working on the quiz. Self-starting was easily maintained by positive reinforcement, such as praising or awarding points to those students who started on their own time. From then on, we needed to make certain preparations in the classroom prior to the students' arrival. The quiz or whatever the self-starting assignment was for that day had to be written on the board and the paper already passed out. We were always in the room to observe and reinforce the self-starting behavior, and, of course, we evaluated the students' efforts often enough to give appropriate value to the assignment.

Having followed this self-starting procedure for a few years, we have found it to be an invaluable tool in two areas: The first is classroom management and control. The fact that the students come into the room with a purpose eliminates much of the behavioral problems that occur when the students have nothing to do. The second is that it provides an excellent opportunity for overlearning of basic concepts. Self-starting, when properly implemented and maintained, can give the students a chance to achieve success and to can give the students a chance to achieve success and to master acquired skills. We are firmly convinced that this one management technique can eliminate about 90 percent of all discipline problems.

CHAPTER V

Four Important Considerations in Classroom Management

Good behavior is no accident. By being aware of the factors that tend to bring about desirable behavior, teachers can literally make their own good day. The four factors to be considered are:

1. Keep the students busy
2. Have a plan for the disruptive students
3. Have two or three simple rules
4. Avoid arguing with the students

1. Keep them busy.

Have you ever noticed how quiet the students are during a test? Probably the main reason for this peaceful, quiet atmosphere is that they are busy doing something they can do. If you keep students busy enough, they won't have time or inclination to engage in improper conduct. Of course, keeping the students busy means more than just piling on assignments. The students must be able to appropriately respond to the task assigned.

There are three critical areas to consider as you work to involve your students in meaningful activities. One of these areas takes place when they are learning a new concept or skill. This we call the "input phase." The second one occurs when the students are involved in an activity that helps them practice a skill or over-learn the concept. We call this the "seat work" phase. The last area is the one that is often overlooked by teachers. It is that time when the students have finished their seat work and are waiting for the teacher to begin new instruction. We call this area the "when finished phase."

Input Phase

In the "input phase," when it is so important to have the class listening and learning, the "silent response" technique can be very effective. By "silent response" we mean that the students give some signal, write something down, or otherwise let the teacher know that they have thought about what has been said or demonstrated. For example, a math teacher could put an eight digit number on the board such as 87,569,134. He could then ask the class to show by their fingers under their chins the number in the thousand's place. The students who know the answer would hold up nine fingers. The key to the "silent response" is to have responses that are quick and simple so that all the students can participate in one way or another. Also, the method of responding should prevent the students from merely showing the same response as their neighbors. It should be a response that is non-threatening to the students if they make a wrong response. Fingers under the chin, response cards, or just a piece of paper placed so only the teacher can see are all excellent ways of involving the students during the input phase. Some teachers in the primary grades have reported good results by asking children to draw a picture of a happy face if they think a statement is correct and a frowning face if the statement is false. The students are told to cover their drawings until the teacher comes around or to show them to the teacher in front of their bodies. Possibly they could put a question mark if they didn't know. The important thing is that students are thinking and actively engaged in the learning situation, and the teacher can receive an immediate feedback as to the effectiveness of the instruction.

A second cousin to the "silent response" is the "no hands" activity. Would you believe that when you ask students *not* to raise their hands you get greater involvement? The technique is called "no hands," and the students are forced into a waiting posture by not allowing them to know who will be called next. Therefore, when a question is asked, everyone will have to find an answer. No one can afford the luxury of mentally dropping out as many tend to do who don't raise their hands under ordinary circumstances. It differs from the ordinary questioning techniques in two respects: the students are not allowed to raise their hands, and the person whose name is called must respond immediately.

In the traditional method of class discussion, the teacher asks for responses from anyone who will volunteer the information. What usually happens in a class of thirty students? Invariably, about ten students will raise their hands. These are students who have thought about the question and feel they have the answer. Another ten may have the answer but really don't care or are shy about responding. The last one third have not listened to the question or thought about the answer because they have been allowed to tune out. They are literally in Dreamsville. So what happens when the next question is posed by the teacher? Typically, the same stars come forth; the shy are allowed to keep their light under the bushel; and the other third's dreams are getting better all the time.

The main advantage of this technique is that all students are literally forced into thinking about the problem or subject under discussion since they don't know who is going to be selected. The only acceptable response is either a direct answer or "I don't know." (The "I don't know" response is not accepted from any one student on a continual basis.) A reasonable amount of time must be given between the asking of the question and the calling of the name so the student will have time to formulate an answer. Because of the forced involvement, more learning takes place by all of the students, and the chance of disruptive behavior is greatly reduced.

The "in-waiting" procedure will follow the steps for "Letting Students Know" adapted from the approach outlined in Chapter II.

1. *Explain the procedure to students:* Simply tell the students that in the future when the teacher asks a question and says "no hands," they are to think about the answer and be ready to respond immediately.

2. *Demonstrate the procedure:* Select two or three students and have them show the rest of the class the correct way to respond, i.e., not raising hands and answering right away.

3. *Practice with the class:* Ask easy questions that can be answered by any of the students. (Emphasis should be on the establishment of the habit of instant response – not learning – in this phase.)

4. *Maintain the procedure:* Students will require constant positive reinforcement at the beginning to insure that the habit is firmly established.

This technique is not intended to replace normal discussion sessions where the raising of hands is encouraged. It is an alternative to be used when the teacher wants total involvement from all members of the class.

One precaution should be observed when using this procedure. The teacher will need to use discretion in calling on students who would be unduly threatened by being required to perform in front of the class. In practice we have found that as the students become accustomed to this technique, the threatening aspect is greatly reduced.

This procedure can be applied to every part of the curriculum and can be used in almost all teaching techniques. The use of "no hands" will bring the students who spend the discussion time in Dreamsville back to the real world.

Seat Work Phase

In this area we have an almost sure-fire way of making certain all the students can and will do the assignment. This technique we call "making sure." Having the students prove they can do the work before the teacher allows them to do it assures more learning and eliminates much of the frustration for both pupil and teacher. Typically, the teacher makes what he/she considers a clear, easily understood presentation – and it probably is – only to have the students begin the independent assignment utilizing the concepts and then find they cannot do it. The teacher is deluged with questions. He/she is frustrated because all the questions can't be answered, and the students are frustrated because they can't go on until they are answered.

There are two major reasons why teachers have this problem. One is that students, knowing their questions will be answered later on, don't listen closely enough to understand the assignment when the instruction is initially given. The other reason is that the teacher's instruction may not be as clear as it appears to be. The procedure of not allowing students to do any work before they prove to the teacher they can do it, is psychologically one of the best motivational factors in the learning process. The steps of this procedure are: first, make sure the presentation is clear; second, have the students do enough samples of the assignment to assure they understand; third, screen the students to allow those who can do the assignment to go to their seats and do it while those who cannot remain with the teacher to receive further instruction.

As with any other technique in this book, this method is applicable in all areas of the curriculum where independent work is assigned. The following is an example that might be used with intermediate levels of instruction in the language arts area:

Words To Be Used:

A. grab	B. scream	C. slight
grate	scrub	slip
grasp	scrape	slimy
grape	scratch	slit

Instructions:

Explain the alphabetizing principle to the fourth letter, i.e., if first three letters are the same then you go to the fourth letter. On this exercise the students will circle the word that would come right after the underlined word.

1. Do Item A with the entire class. "Which word comes after the underlined word?" Discuss why.

2. Next the class does Item B without discussion. Find out how many chose each word. "How many chose scrub (Point to that word.) . . . scrape . . . scratch?" Discuss as necessary.

3. After the discussion of the reasons for the correct answer of Item B, the class does Item C independently. The teacher circulates and checks to see which students understand the exercise and which ones need further help. The students who understand are allowed to do their independent seat work. Those who don't are given additional instruction.

Another technique we have found very useful in assuring that students do seat work promptly and completely is called "add on way." The beauty of this technique is that the students not only do the work with enthusiasm but learn a complicated concept and retain it. The secret is to teach a small section at a time for mastery and review it at the next instructional period for retention.

For example, we would teach the map of the United States in this way. On the first day, students would be given a piece of paper that they would prepare for four days' use. (See Figures 1, 2, 3, 4.) The students would be led through the boundaries including the Great Lakes. They would then be expected to draw that from memory. On the second day, the students would begin the assignment that was given for the first day by reproducing boundary lines, and the new information would be the four major mountain ranges.

On the third day the students would begin the assignment by reproducing the boundaries and the major mountain ranges while the new information would be the five major rivers. Keep in mind that the beginning review of each day's assignment must be done from memory without teacher help.

On the fourth day the students would begin the assignment by reproducing the boundary lines, major mountain ranges, and major rivers on their own, and the new information this day would be the major cities.

The idea is to give them the amount of information they can assimilate and still retain what they've already learned.

The frosting on the cake from using this method is that we've had many students come back to us years later bragging that they were able to draw these maps letter perfect. And they could!

We would use the same system for teaching the physiology of the ear as it relates to hearing. The paper would be prepared for four days. (See Figures 5, 6, 7, 8.) The first day we would present the outer ear. The students would then draw it from memory. On the second day, they would review the outer ear from memory as their beginning assignment, and the new information would be the middle ear. On the

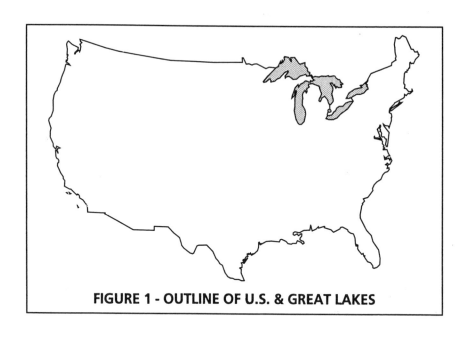

FIGURE 1 - OUTLINE OF U.S. & GREAT LAKES

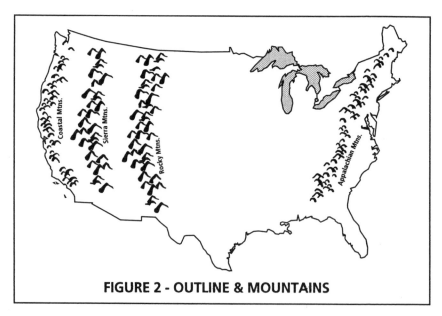

FIGURE 2 - OUTLINE & MOUNTAINS

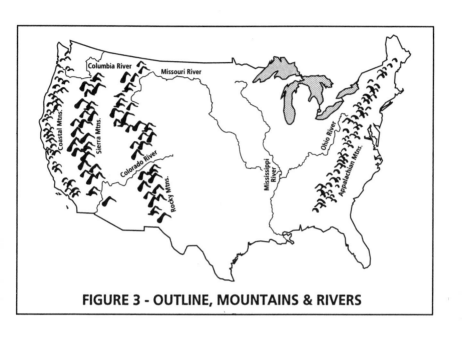

FIGURE 3 - OUTLINE, MOUNTAINS & RIVERS

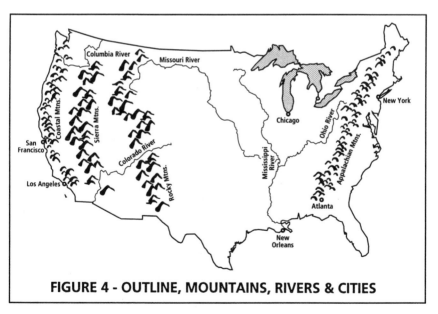

FIGURE 4 - OUTLINE, MOUNTAINS, RIVERS & CITIES

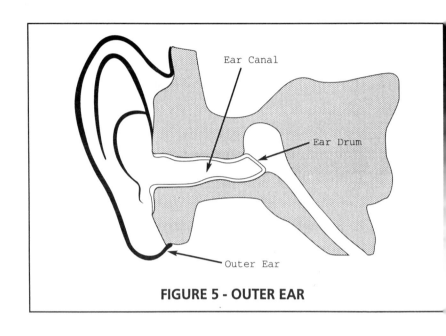

FIGURE 5 - OUTER EAR

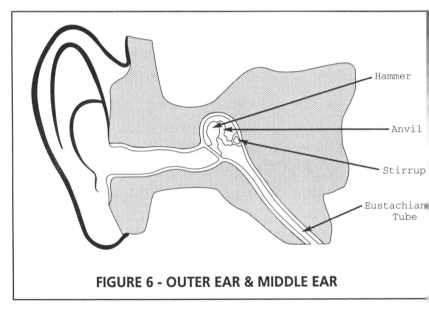

FIGURE 6 - OUTER EAR & MIDDLE EAR

38

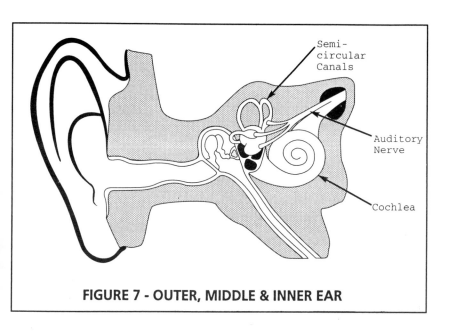

FIGURE 7 - OUTER, MIDDLE & INNER EAR

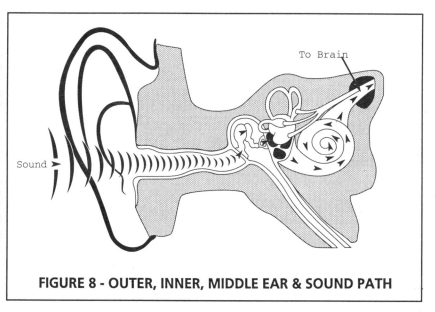

FIGURE 8 - OUTER, INNER, MIDDLE EAR & SOUND PATH

third day, the new chunk of information would be the inner ear, and on the fourth day would be the refinement such as the path sound travels through the ear until the message reaches the brain. Bear in mind that each instructional period begins with the student drawing from memory the pieces of information already presented in preparation for the new material. On the fifth day, we would have a test to determine mastery of this concept.

The ease and speed with which students learn and retain concepts using the add-on method is truly astounding. Even more satisfying to the teacher is the enjoyment the students seem to display when they can demonstrate to their teachers, peers, and parents the mastery of an extremely difficult task such as drawing a map of the world and putting in all important features like oceans, mountain ranges, rivers, major nations, and capitals – all from memory! The key point to remember in this method is to make sure they recreate that which they have learned the previous day or days before adding new concepts or skills.

When Finished Phase

One of the most challenging times for any teacher is when some of the students are finished and others are not. We have heard this referred to as "the awkward moments" and indeed it is. Ideally, the assignment would be one so that all students would finish at the same time. But, realistically, even in an ability grouped classroom, the students will finish at different times. Many control problems happen during these "awkward moments." The obvious solution to the problem is to have something for them to do and make sure they understand the procedure to be followed so that minimum distraction occurs when they do it. Among the many activities that teachers have used in keeping students busy during this "when finished" phase are: on-going projects, games and puzzles, and a general instruction.

An on-going project can be one the students do for several days in a row. Art projects, knitting a hat, and bead pictures are a few that we have observed teachers using. These activities require some guidelines to be observed by the students. It may be worthwhile to go through the four-step procedure in Chapter II, "Letting Them Know." The amount of preparation given the students will depend on their maturity level. At any rate, they will need to understand: where and when to obtain supplies and tools, the behavior needed to prevent distractions, and how to return the supplies and project to the proper place. A practice session may be worthwhile to ensure smooth operation. Students will need to know the procedure to follow if they need help. A simple rule of not seeking teacher's help if he/she is helping another student will be helpful.

The games and puzzles activities need little teacher attention. Some preparation will be required to make sure that the games and puzzles are accessible. Once again the limits to behavior need to be explained. Certainly loud raucous laughter or shouting should be included in these limits. One teacher uses objects found in her house. She places these in a large box, and the children play creative games with them. Of course, the items must be harmless.

Another method of keeping youngsters busy during an "awkward moment" is to have a general instruction for everybody to follow when they finish. This seems to work well for the upper grades. The instruction could go something like this, "Whenever you finish an assignment in this class, you can read for recreation, do your homework for this class or others, or you may do anything that will not disturb others who are not finished." The last activity will probably require a little explanation or brainstorming to clarify the activities that would be included in the disturbing activities.

Keeping the students busy when they finish is of extreme importance to the teacher in controlling the class.

If this can be accomplished with a minimum of time and effort, all the better. The students need to have a clear idea of the activities they can do when finished and the behavioral expectations during the activity. The overriding rule should be that they won't disturb the class during this critical time. There will be times, of course, that the teacher will use activities that have no learning, and this is fine. But if students can keep busy and learn something while doing it, it is even better.

2. Have a plan.

Knowing ahead what you will do in the event of certain misbehavior will allow you to act with confidence, make better decisions, and usually solve the problems.

Those behaviors you may want to plan ahead for are: open defiance, fighting, the nonworking student, and the extremely disruptive child. The teacher decides on certain steps to be taken in connection with each unacceptable behavior. The steps must be clear in the teacher's mind so that he/she can take action with complete confidence and quiet self-assurance. This confidence by itself is almost enough to assure success in dealing with the problem.

For example, when we go on a field trip, we have a plan. First, we make it very clear what behavior is acceptable and what is not. We let the students know that unacceptable behavior will result in the student's being brought back to the school and given normal work for the rest of the day. A teacher is assigned to drive a car to the place of the field trip and bring the offender back to school; hence, it is very easy to do what you have said you will do. This not only takes care of the specific child who is misbehaving, but acts as a deterrent to others who may think of misbehaving. The student knows that the teacher will follow through and that it will not be any great problem for the teacher to do so.

The car that is meant to be used to bring the students back is very seldom used. In fact, student behavior has been exemplary because the plan for dealing with possible misbehavior is easily executed.

Another example of having a plan is in dealing with the extremely disruptive child. Here again, examine some of the things you find objectionable in the child's conduct and then make a step-by-step plan for dealing with these things. Next "pave the way." By this we mean to set up the machinery so that the execution of the plan becomes relatively simple and almost automatic. If suspension is imminent (when the entire class is unable to function or learn because of this one child), then it is best to let the parents know that this action is a distinct possibility. Also, the principal should be advised of the situation. Above all, the student should be aware of your plan and be aware of your firm intention to carry it out. When you conference with the student (you may want the parents present), point out the exact nature of the unacceptable conduct and specify clearly what will happen if he or she does not follow the expectations.

Probably the single most important aspect of having a plan is the effect it has upon you, the teacher. If you react to a student in the typical manner, (i.e., student misbehaves, teacher decides immediately how to correct the student and takes action) the result is not usually productive. For one thing, you may act from emotion and make some decision or take some action that you may later regret. But if your action is the result of reflective thought, it will take into consideration the child, the importance of his action, and a method of correcting it. You have, in fact, given yourself a course of action to follow that will allow you to work with calmness, assuredness, and clarity when the problem arises.

3. Have two or three simple rules.

It would be nice to have enough rules to cover every single situation that could possibly occur and be able to strictly enforce them. However, the realities and complexities of school life will not allow this. The best solution is to select two or three simple rules that can be enforced and that are deemed necessary to conduct an orderly classroom. The rules need to be acceptable to the students and to you.

In realizing that we cannot expect every student to behave the way we ideally would like them to at all times, the selection process for the critical rules is very important. The rules should be the ones most closely connected to basic classroom control. The other rules which are not deemed so critical for control can be set aside as being "nice to have" but not essential. The enforcement of these rules can be more flexible. An example of a rule that would not be critical to classroom control would be: "Do not let any paper fall on the floor." Some teachers may wish to have this rule and others may not, depending on how much the litter on the floor bothers them. The point is that a rule regarding paper on the floor is desirable from the standpoint of housekeeping, but will not in itself make a significant difference in the degree of control a teacher has. On the other hand, the critical rules that you intend to rigorously enforce should be ones that really help in maintaining good control. Good control is that condition in the classroom where the behavior of students is acceptable to you with due regard for the rights of students to learn without undue distraction and also with due regard for the rights of other teachers in the building. Consider for a moment the noise level of your class. Is it too noisy for your own peace of mind and is it distracting to the students? If the answer is "yes," then a rule that will decrease the noise would be advisable and that would be one of the two or three essential rules. But if the noise level is not a problem to you and the students seem to be able to learn in the class without distraction, then this would mean that a rule to keep the noise down would not be one of the critical ones.

For our own particular situation, we have three critical

rules. They were chosen to help us get and maintain control with consideration given to our students, our mode of operation, and our teachers in the team. The rules are:

1. Raise hands before talking to the class.
2. Give teacher attention on signal.
3. Self-start at beginning of class.

We introduce the rules to the class on the first day. They are explained, demonstrated, and practiced until the behavior is internalized. We are non-permissive in enforcing these rules. We do not work on the other behaviors or rules until the essential ones have been thoroughly mastered.

4. Avoid arguing.

Allowing the students to argue with you is nonproductive and detrimental to good control. It is up to the teacher to make certain constructive discussions occur rather than arguing and bickering.

Whenever the teacher becomes involved in a position where both he/she and the student are displaying anger and yelling back and forth without really listening to each other, you can safely assume there is arguing instead of productive discussion. On the other hand, students do need an avenue to express their points of view. When an orderly process is established, allowing free exchange without undue emotion, control in the class is enhanced. Furthermore, students learn a valuable lesson – that much more can be gained by calmly presenting a point of view using the power of logic instead of the power of the voice.

You can avoid falling into the trap of arguing by simply refusing to respond to the student's yelling and shouting. Teachers who become engaged in shouting matches with students are those who in most cases are willing to engage in them. The best way to insure that calmness and reason prevail in the class is to be calm and reasonable. Also, you need to make certain that you are receptive to reasonable entreaty and that the students understand that a way is open for expression of opinions and ideas if proper restraint is exercised.

Instead of arguing with your students, we suggest two courses of action. One is that you may want to postpone any discussion to a more appropriate time and the other is that you may feel that the matter is urgent enough to be discussed immediately. If you decide to discuss it right away, the procedure to facilitate orderly discussion must be established. First, insist that only *one person talk at a time.* Second, insist that both parties, you and the student or students, *listen to each other.*

Postponing the discussion until a later time has some advantages. Not only do you have more time to prepare the students involved for the orderly process of reasoning as opposed to arguing, but the intemperate atmosphere present during an argument is usually diminished. If you promise the students that you will discuss it later, be sure that you keep that promise.

A constant use of this approach for avoiding arguments with your students can be a factor in preserving good control in your classroom.

CHAPTER VI

The Voice

Possibly the single most important factor in maintaining control is the voice of the teacher. Your voice can cause the students to listen or not to listen. A teacher who is willing to find out what a "good classroom voice" is and is willing to take the time to develop one, can almost be assured of good control – without doing anything else. The main purpose of this chapter is to draw your attention to the importance of the voice and present a few hints or techniques that you can use to help you have a "good classroom voice."

The Importance of the Voice

The importance of the voice cannot be overstated. In observing teachers, we have found that too few are aware of the tremendous effect the voice has upon students' behavior. Most of them are unaware of the immense potential that their voice could have in better control. Oddly enough, the universities and the colleges involved with teacher education do very little to help future teachers to use their voice more effectively.

The teacher can literally draw the students into a cone of control and persuade them to cooperate simply by using a good classroom voice. The way it is said far outweighs the words used to say it. The voice also has a decided effect on the restlessness of the class. The high-pitched, tense, or strident voice tends to induce restlessness, whereas the calm and measured voice tends to induce calmness in the class.

Not to be overlooked is the effect the voice has upon its user. You can actually calm yourself by speaking in a calm, reassuring manner. Supervisors of sales clerks use this technique to help their personnel. They tell them that if they find themselves getting upset to try greeting their customers with a smile. It really works. Their day brightens and so can yours by getting your voice where you wish your emotions were – calm and reassured.

What is a good classroom voice?

Our definition of a "good classroom voice" is one that causes students to listen and learn and one that is appropriate to the activity at hand. Generally speaking, we have found that there are two aspects of the voice that cause students to listen and respond. One is a soft, controlled voice and the other is the practice of lowering the voice at the end of a sentence.

A soft voice means one with the absence of high shrill tones. This "good" voice is down in the lower part of your voice register. A controlled voice is one that is paced so as not to speak too rapidly – just fast enough to maintain interest.

Lowering the voice at the end of a sentence seems to do two things. It forces others to listen to you, and it forces you to use the self-controlled voice for the entire sentence. Notice how the best speakers (the ones whom you feel compelled to listen to) and most of the broadcasters come down at the end of their sentences. They are using a technique that forces one to listen to them, and you can use this technique to gain your students' attention.

How to Develop the Good Classroom Voice

Developing the type of voice that is so important in control will take very little effort on your part. There are things you can do in your daily activities in the class that will not take extra time or effort. First, just being aware of your voice and its potential is a very big help. As soon as you realize that by bringing the voice down you will bring the students' attention up, you will tend to do so.

It is a good idea to practice good classroom voice techniques in non-threatening situations. When you call the roll, you can drop the voice on the last syllable. As you read or give instructions to your class, drop the voice at the end of each instruction. Spelling tests also provide an opportunity to practice lowering your voice. As you give each word, come down at the end. Telling stories, reading to the class, etc., can all be used for this purpose. It is important that you practice enough to make it habitual. For those who are really intent on mastering the "good" voice, tape recorders can be used with good results.

We feel that the voice is so important, we would say that if you can implement the suggestions in this chapter, you will definitely have better classroom control, even though you were to ignore the rest of the book.

CHAPTER VII

Random Ideas on Control

The amount of noise and movement that you allow your class will vary from one activity to another. You certainly would not expect the class to be as quiet in physical education class as you would during a math test. Activities such as puppet shows, creative dramatics, and role-playing will require a greater tolerance on the part of the teacher for the spontaneous expression that is desired in these activities. The important thing is that you are able to recognize that some activities do require more noise and movement than others and that you can and must have some way of keeping the noise and movement from becoming excessive.

Don't turn them on unless you can turn them off.

There are many activities of high excitement that you can have without havoc. In fact, none of the innovative activities associated with creative learning should be shunned for fear of losing class control. Learning through discussion, learning centers, modular scheduling, planning one's own schedules, etc., should be part of your curriculum if you desire them. If the students are fully prepared so that they have the habit of staying on task and if you have confidence that you can bring the class back to absolute quiet with literally a "snap of the fingers," then you need not eliminate any learning method from the curriculum. The key is, *don't turn them on unless you can turn them off.*

Regardless of the activity, there should always be a framework of control present, if not always apparent. This framework will give the teacher a means of giving the students plenty of freedom without the chaos that often leads to premature abandonment of a worthwhile project.

An example of how the class can function within this control framework without having the teacher lose sanity can be found in one of our favorite science projects. We have the students work in groups of four to plan and produce a poster on air pollution. The purpose of the poster is to inform others of the value of clean air and help to develop a positive attitude toward clean air by the groups. We prepare our students by telling them the purpose of the assignment, reminding them of certain behavioral expectations, and giving them training in group process skills. Since we have been developing good behavioral habits in the children from the first of the year, we need to spend very little time structuring their behavior. The most valuable asset in attempting this project is our confidence that we can restore order any time the noise level exceeds our expectation.

If you don't have control – stop teaching!

We once worked with a teacher whose class was out of control to the point that the other teachers in the unit could not function. When she sought help, we suggested she stop teaching. By this we did not mean she should quit her job as a teacher, but she should stop trying to teach the class anything except how to behave. She should work primarily and completely on control. This was to be her first and only priority. This teacher stopped the learning activity and focused on classroom management procedures by:

1. Holding a very serious group meeting where she explained the type of behavior that was acceptable and the type that was not acceptable.
2. Demonstrating the acceptable behavior.
3. Practicing the behavior.
4. Evaluating the behavior.

As we indicated in the first chapter, the time spent in gaining (or regaining) control will be paid back many times in accelerated learning once the class is listening and staying on task. This concept should be employed any time it is applicable and not just at the first of the year.

During the time required to restore control, which could be one hour or one week, there probably will be work assignments and lessons, but the objective will focus on control rather than the usual subject matter. If subject matter learning takes place, this is fine and good; but if none takes place, this also is acceptable, knowing that more content learning will take place eventually and understanding that for the time being the greatest lessons the children and teacher can master have to do with classroom control.

The Preparedness Panacea

One of the most common bits of advice given to new teachers is that, if you are well prepared, you will experience few control problems. While we readily agree that there is no substitute for adequate preparation, this in itself will not guarantee control. We have observed teachers who spent hours in preparation, gave faultless presentations, and taught nothing. The learning was minimal because the students simply were not listening and would not participate in the learning activities. We firmly believe the amount of time spent in preparation will only pay off if the students have the habits of proper behavior. Those habits are: listening when the teacher is talking, not distracting others, and getting on task and staying on it until the task is complete. Once again, we are not downgrading the importance of preparation; it is an essential part of excellence in teaching. We merely wish to point out that the basic tenents of control must be observed to maximize learning.

Futility of Moralizing

Too often teachers try to elicit better behavior by appealing to the basic goodness of their students and seeking their sympathy. This type of "moralizing" usually has little effect and is short-lived. In fact, it may diminish the respect for the teacher since the students may perceive him/her as lacking control to the point where he/she has to plead or beg. The simple truth is, very few teachers effectively maintain control by constantly remonstrating and entreating. The reason for this is simple; the students who already have acceptable behavior are usually the ones who respond, while the ones who don't, tend to ignore the appeals. However, this does not mean that you shouldn't try to explain or discuss behavior with your students. A group discussion can be very valuable in helping students understand why one behavior is permitted while another is not.

Being Friendly but Maintaining Dignity

Since classes vary so much in their general behavior and teachers vary so much in their ability to effectively control their classes, it is difficult to give any rule about how friendly to be toward your class or whether you should be friends with individual members of the class. About the best advice we can give is never to be so friendly with the students that you lose your role as a teacher.

Teachers, especially new teachers, should be aware of certain irrevocable mistakes. These mistakes are the type that by-and-large you cannot remedy in the middle of the year. You have to wait until you have a new class at the beginning of the next year. A frequent irrevocable mistake is one of becoming overly friendly without considering your ability to maintain your status as a teacher as well as the class's ability to cope with this familiarity. Getting to be friends or buddies with the students can have some real pitfalls. Some students simply are not mature enough to revert back to the role of a student when it is necessary for class control. This can result in alienation of the students when the teacher seems to betray their friendship by being stern or authoritative. Therefore, it is best to be on the cautious side and avoid being overly friendly until you are certain the students can handle it.

CHAPTER VIII

Punishment

Good classroom management procedures should eliminate almost all need for punishment; however, there are times when punishment may be necessary. Punishment can be effective in maintaining control if the teacher understands what punishment really is, what precautions need to be taken in using mass punishment, and what guidelines need to be observed in using any type of punishment.

What is punishment?

For clarification we will define punishment as something unpleasant for the student and something that has the purpose of correcting the student's behavior. The "unpleasant" aspect of punishment is basically something that the student does not like. This may vary from student to student. The other aspect, that of "correcting," refers to modifying or possibly changing a behavior that is unacceptable. In other words, the unpleasantness must be closely enough associated with the unacceptable behavior to effectively prevent recurrence of the unacceptable behavior. Any action on the part of the teacher that does not satisfy these two conditions, unpleasant and corrective, will not be considered as punishment under this stipulated definition.

Many teachers err in using punishment because they do not realize that the punishment they administer may not be that unpleasant for a particular child. What is unpleasant for one may be pleasant for another. For instance, the little girl who is kept in for recess in cold weather may, in fact, really enjoy staying in. Or "isolating" two or three students at the same time in a room to eat their lunch together for misbehavior in the lunch room, could prove to be no punishment at all. They may have the time of their lives. So the first concern of the teacher in applying punishment when it becomes necessary is to be aware of what exactly is unpleasant to the individual student being punished. If you really need to use punishment, make certain it is something the child does not like.

Does punishment work?

Many experts in the field of education admonish us against the use of punishment on the grounds that it does not work. We take the position that this is nonsense. Punishment that is prudently applied along with good classroom management procedures can and does work. However, punishment by itself as the only tool to be used in class control would definitely be a mistake and would justify the criticism of the experts. On the other hand, it would be equally a mistake to think that all teachers can survive in a real classroom, as opposed to the ideal, without occasionally resorting to punishment or the threat of punishment.

Punishment can be used to help a specific child to refrain from repeating a disruptive act. However, a much greater value in using punishment is the effect it has on those who are not being punished. Knowing that a certain consequence results from a specific unacceptable act is frequently more effective for the entire class than it is for the one or two violators. This deterrent effect of punishment exists on two different levels, the conscious and the subconscious. Students do not take part in unacceptable activities because they do not want to be punished (conscious), and they shy away from the stigma of being classified as an offender (subconscious).

The question presents itself as to when we need to use punishment. The answer will depend on three variables: the teacher, the students, and the program. It may be that some teachers, with a particular group of students and their abilities, may never need to resort to punishment. Other teachers may need to use punishment fairly often. At any rate, punishment should never be used more often than necessary for the given conditions. The more sparingly it is used, the more effective it will become. As a general rule, you will resort to punishment when all else fails. Any teacher who has taught for any length of time will in all probability have encountered a child who does not respond to positive measures. If the only alternative left is punishment, then it must be used if the rights of others to learn are to be protected.

Punishment can also be considered in relation to giving positive reinforcement. For instance, in the self-starting activities we have used over the years, we have occasionally used a mild form of punishment for a few who would not begin work when they sat down in their seats. We would merely have them come in and practice self-starting during the recess or after school. (We would like to point out that this was rarely necessary since most of the students responded to praise.) In every instance this punishment was effective in encouraging those particular students to self-start. The interesting fact about this is that the rest of the class was immediately placed in the reward zone. First, they were rewarded by not being punished and, secondly, they could consider themselves as part of an elite group who were self-directed. We always explained to the students that there are basically two groups of students – those who can follow directions after they have been told once, and those who seem to need extra drill and practice to be able to do things right. The amazing thing is that very seldom is there anyone in the latter group because everybody wants to be identified as being in the "once only" group. It is necessary to carry through with the practice sessions once in a while to allow the students to feel rewarded for doing things right.

Mass Punishment

We are opposed to mass punishment for two reasons. The first is that it is not so effective as other forms and the second is that it is patently unfair.

Mass punishment most often results in a division in which the teacher is in one camp and the students are in another – the one thing you want to avoid in classroom control. In fact, the students in the class who have been behaving are often discouraged because they see no benefit for good behavior.

Moreover, even if it were effective, we still would not condone its use because it is unfair to most of the students. If the class comes in noisily, and the teacher sends the entire class outside to come in quietly, this teacher is probably being unfair to someone. It would be very unusual if at least one student wasn't coming in properly. Admittedly, recognizing the few who are not noisy can be very difficult, but it can be done. The teacher merely observes the class with this purpose in mind, that is, to identify those who behave, or, if easier, those who misbehave. In separating the few who come into the class without disturbing, you can clarify your expectations to the others. Of course, it would be much better if the students knew in advance what your expectations were and that the "practice to learn" procedure is the natural consequence of not coming in properly. For those times when it is impossible to separate those who behave from those who don't, we recommend that no punishment be used. It is best to wait for the next occurrence when you can take the measures necessary to make accurate observations and to make sure that the class knows expectations.

Probably the greatest abuse involving mass punishment occurs because the teachers do not know when they are using this form of punishment. Teachers who admit that mass punishment is grossly unfair employ it all the time without realizing they are doing so. Some subtle forms of mass punishment are: berating the entire class for the misbehavior of a few; making the class members miss their regular turn at some activity or lose their regular turn to go to lunch; keeping the whole class in for recess or dismissing them late. Take the case of a teacher who tells the class, "We won't be going home until all the scraps are off the floor." Although this teacher may deny that he/she ever uses mass punishment, he/she is, nevertheless, using it. The non-mass punishment way would be to say, "Those students who have trash under their desks will need to stay until their area is clean" or "The student leader will dismiss the students whose areas are clean." This is not only more fair, but if consistently used can be much more effective.

There is, however, one reason for using mass punishment – i.e., if that's the only recourse you have. If it's the only thing you have going for you, by all means use it rather than having chaos. At any rate, use it only until you can develop better alternatives.

Guidelines for Use of Punishment

When punishment becomes necessary one should follow these four guidelines:

1. The punishment should be appropriate for the offense.
2. Non-constructive punishment should be avoided.
3. Denying the privilege of working is probably the best punishment.
4. For extreme cases the offender should be isolated.

The appropriateness of punishment refers to matching the severity of punishment with the seriousness of the offense. The danger in using punishment that is too severe is that it tends to alienate the student to the point where all future efforts for constructive behavioral changes are thwarted. Most often a very mild form of punishment can be just as effective, and the respect of the student for the teacher is not diminished. Also, where the milder form of punishment is employed, the resulting psychological climate insures that the student is receptive to an explanation as to why the punishment is necessary – a very necessary aspect of any punishment. A rule of thumb would be that except for extreme cases, "The best is the least."

A form of punishment that is not constructive (that which is not effective in producing the results you want, or that which has more undesirable effects than desirable) is assigning extra school work. For instance, copying a page out of the dictionary may be counter-productive. It may be no punishment at all for many students who really like to copy things or if the student hates the task he may learn to hate the dictionary as well. Make certain that the punishment doesn't have the side effect of promoting a negative attitude toward any aspect of the classroom learning situations.

On the other hand, we have found that denying to students the privilege of working can be very effective. By and large, most children (and adults) prefer to be engaged in some activity.

As a last resort, for extreme cases, isolation will sometimes need to be used. Isolation has two uses: It removes the offender so the class can carry on without the disturbance, and it serves the purpose of being the most severe form of punishment. But remember that putting two people together is not isolating. If you have two children misbehaving in the lunchroom, it is far better to have them eat their lunches where they cannot communicate with anyone – especially with each other. For the most flagrant cases, the teacher should not be adverse to recommending suspension from school. Here again, "paving the way" by notifying the people concerned of your recommendation will make it much easier to carry out the threat.

Summary

As distasteful as punishment may seem, reality necessitates its use at times. It has been and can be effective if you use it judiciously so that it does not alienate the student from the teacher and the school, and if it serves as a corrective measure for those who are misbehaving and as a deterrent to those who are not.

CHAPTER IX

When Punishment Fails

The approach we've used so far in the book tends to reduce control problems to a manageable level. However, there will often be two or three students who require more individual help than has been described. The chart on the following page shows the steps a teacher might take to filter the class down to these few students.

Usually, students who do not respond to the normal range of teacher interventions rely on external controls. The challenge then is to change their control from external to internal, i.e., the ability to recognize inappropriate behavior and adjust it accordingly. In this chapter we will discuss a practice that has helped a number of these students develop an internal control over their behavior. Of course, there may be a time when intervention by others, such as the principal, pupil support team, and parents, will be required. We have found the one-on-one conferencing procedure to be effective with these few students.

Conferencing with the Individual Student

It is important at the beginning of a conference to establish a certain physical and psychological setting so the student is convinced that both he and the teacher are working

Usual Progression in Reducing Problems

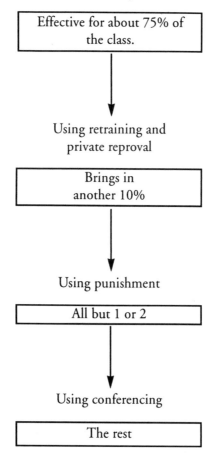

Using methods suggested in ear-
lier chapters such as self-starting,
class meetings, voice, keeping
students busy, etc.

Effective for about 75% of
the class.

Using retraining and
private reproval

Brings in
another 10%

Using punishment

All but 1 or 2

Using conferencing

The rest

together to solve the problem. In order to accomplish this, a time must be selected in which there is no discord between you and the student. This insures that both you and the student are operating from the rational part of your brain rather than the emotional. The teacher and student sitting side by side is an important factor in establishing a collaborative feeling instead of the confrontational feeling that arises when they are sitting across from each other or the teacher is physically higher than the student.

The way the teacher opens the conference is critical to helping the student develop self-awareness and to take responsibility for his/her own actions. The student must be convinced that the teacher is there in a helping role – not an adversarial one. Comments such as, "Nick, you're really causing me problems in this classroom" or "John, do you realize that you're stopping other children from learning?" tend to create resistance in the student. A better opening is, "Nick, I notice you're having a difficult time lately. I'd like to help you change that," because it invites the student to enter into a partnership with you.

Since our goal is to help the student look at his behavior, the question must be framed to cause him to examine those behaviors he has that create problems. Questions such as, "Nick, as you think back on your last week in school, what kinds of things do you see yourself doing that create problems for you?" Notice that Nick is asked the question in such a way that he is prompted to look objectively at his behavior and to start to accept responsibility for it. At this point, the teacher's role shifts from that of initiating the question to listening and recording Nick's answers. Typical responses that students give are: "I talk back to you." "When Gina bugs me, I bug her back." "I forget my pencil and can't start my work." "When other kids push me, I push them back." While the answers have some element of blame in them, these responses are terrific progress in the shift from external to internal controls. There may be times when it is appropriate to nudge a student into expanding the list. But you'll want to keep this to a minimum. Keep in mind that the main purpose of this conference is to keep a positive atmosphere and *to get the student to look at his behavior.*

Once the initial list is made, the student is invited to select two behaviors that, if changed, would provide a more successful school experience. Then the teacher selects one of these. This gives the student control over his destiny while preserving the teacher's input on his behavioral changes. Some examples of goals students have chosen are:

1. Avoid arguing with the teacher

2. Avoid taking other students' property

3. Bring pencils or books to class

The single goal teachers typically choose from the list relate to students following directions or starting and remaining on task during work times. Notice these are specific, achievable goals.

Here is an example of a chart that we've used to help students assess their progress on their goals.

INSTRUCTIONS: Rate yourself on a scale of 1-5 on the behaviors listed below.

BEHAVIORS	RATING				

We use a five-point numerical rating system for older students and picture symbols for very young students in this rating chart.

During the last part of the day, the teacher holds a reflective conference with the student at which he is asked to rate his behavior on the stated goals on a scale of one to five with five being nearly perfect and one being very poor indeed. Remembering that the goal is for the student to reflect on his own behavior, the teacher resists the impulse to tell the student how he did. Rather the student is prompted to rate himself and to give reasons why that rating was given. Initially there will be very little progress. And this is to be expected and accepted. Behavior this extreme does not change overnight. It can only begin to change as the student becomes aware of what he is doing and, through a dialogue with the teacher, plans a way to change his behavior.

This process requires great skill and sensitivity from the teacher as he/she helps the student see the progress that has been made and builds on that progress to help the student further refine those behaviors. Two key points are: (1) Always have students explain the reasons why they gave themselves the rating they received. It is in the reason-giving that students begin the process of monitoring their behavior and taking responsibility for changing it. (2) The focus of the conference should be only on the goals set by the teacher and the student. For example, if one of the goals is that the student will avoid arguing with the teacher, only that behavior should be considered in the rating even though the student may have done poorly in other behaviors not stated in the goals. Therefore, it is possible that a high rating could be achieved on "avoid arguing" even though the student may have taken the ball away from another student on the playground. This allows the student to succeed in one area, which is important to him in changing his behavior.

Summary

While in most cases the goal was only to get the student to look at his behavior, the result has been that eight out of ten not only looked at their poor behavior but made significant progress from maladaptive to adaptive behavior. They changed their control from external to internal by developing the ability to recognize inappropriate behavior and adjust it accordingly. Of course, many teachers will not be able to use this procedure with this high degree of success, but we feel that it is worth the try. The following story gives a poignant example:

Chad was a boy who fell into the category of the two or three students for whom punishment failed. He seemed totally removed from classroom activities. When instruction was given, he rummaged around in his desk or took pens apart. Starting on assignments occurred only after he received several promptings from his teacher. He had to be reminded two or three times to line up with the class – even to go to physical education. He became belligerent if the teacher pressed him too hard to complete his work. Even the resource teacher could not get him to function. When the resource teacher and the teacher met with Chad, by chance they asked him if he were worried that he might not make it in junior high. He burst into uncontrollable sobs. After he calmed down, a conference was held with Chad similar to the one described in this chapter. Four goals were set in that conference. Chad would:

1. bring his books and pencils to class,
2. start his work immediately after an assignment was given,
3. line up with the class immediately when called,

4. have his "lights on," which meant he would be alert to and attend to what was happening in the classroom.

Over a six-month period Chad slowly transformed from a "cipher in the snow" to a fully-functioning sixth-grade student with a smile that went from one ear to another. By the end of the year, the only goal Chad evaluated himself on daily was the last one – to have his lights turned on. After he left elementary school, the two teachers were concerned over how he was doing in junior high school. About Christmas time Chad showed up at the elementary school with a wonderful smile and sparkling eyes. The first words out of his mouth were, "Guess what! My lights are still on!"

CHAPTER X

A Principal's Perspective

If you have a genuine concern for children, you must have a genuine concern for discipline. This goes for principals as well as teachers; in fact, the principal usually sets the atmosphere of the school. Just as some teachers are "their own worst enemy" (being the most disruptive factor in the classroom), some principals walk from classroom to classroom upsetting the learning process with their casual manner and thoughtless interruptions. The most delicate and potent relationship in education is when teachers are teaching and students are learning. In view of this, all staff, parents, visitors, and especially the principal, should be aware and appreciative of this and work tenaciously to minimize interruptions. It would be unthinkable to interrupt a surgeon during an operation to discuss a casual matter. Even though the teaching-learning relationship may not directly affect life and death, it does affect something equally precious – the molding and training of the mind and character. Showing a greater respect for the "teaching act" will almost automatically improve classroom control.

Clarifying Areas of Responsibility

At the very first faculty meeting of the year the principal should remove all doubt as to what is expected of the teacher in the matter of classroom control and just what the teacher may expect of the principal.

The teacher is contracted to teach and is expected to be competent in the area of classroom control. The basic responsibility for discipline is the teacher's. Just as a principal should not plague teachers with unnecessary interruptions, teachers should not send students to the office because of minor classroom problems. The principal's office has a more important function than serving as a dumping ground for children you can't control.

Generally, the more the principal becomes involved in the problems of classroom management, the poorer the discipline becomes. Insecure teachers will give up their problems as long as the principal will assume them, but as a result, the teacher ends up having less respect and less authority in the classroom. This will be true even though the principal may be working feverishly for the opposite effect.

The Principal's Area of Responsibility

The principal needs to become involved when a student's behavior involves one of the following situations:

1. Insolence, defiance, or refusal to follow teacher's instructions

2. Act(s) of physical harm to persons or property

3. Immoral conduct, or use of alcohol, tobacco or drugs

4. Cutting class (truancy)

The Teacher's Area of Responsibility

Examples of student offenses that should *not* involve the principal are:

1. Disturbing others or out of seat

2. Cheating, lying, petty stealing

3. Tardiness

4. Gum chewing and eating in class

In general, all classroom problems are to be handled by the teacher with the exception of the "Principal's Area of Responsibility" above. However, if a teacher has a persistent problem with a child, it is expedient to discuss the matter with the principal and/or counselor, psychologist, social worker, fellow teacher. By all means get some good advice on the problem.

Making Referrals to the Principal

On matters involving the "Principal's Area of Responsibility," it is advisable to make a prompt referral to the principal. When taking or sending a student to the principal, communicate to him the specific nature of the student's problem and what, if any, recommendations and expectations you may have. (A sample "Referral to Principal" form is included at the end of this chapter for this purpose.)

When a student arrives at the principal's office*, the principal has at least five options he can use:

Option #1 – Standard Treatment

The student is asked to sit by himself in a room adjacent to the office, preferably with his head down. This serves as a good time for reflection. Within an hour the principal interviews the student obtaining his expression on these two points:

1. What he was doing as opposed to what he was supposed to be doing
2. A sincere intent and commitment to do better in the future

---

* Going to the principal's office for discipline has traditionally caused considerable student anxiety and trauma. Unfortunately, for some students it has now become such a commonplace thing that they may say, "Big deal! What can the principal do, kick me out? Who wants to be in this dumb school anyhow?" We must take whatever safegruards are necessary to restore the dignity and effectiveness of the principal's office.

If all goes well, the student is given an admit to class. However, if these two steps are not achieved to the satisfaction of the principal the student is asked to call his parents and explain his situation. After the student has done this the principal takes the phone and tells the parents the conditions upon which the student may be given an admit to class. If the student still balks, move to option #2.

Option #2 – In-School Suspension

At this point parents are informed that an attitudinal change must take place before the student can be readmitted to class and that you are providing a half-day of "thinking time" at the office for the student to consider what kind of a student he wants to be. No harsh words need to be spoken to the student. He is given courteous silent treatment. At the end of the half-day period the student is given another opportunity to express his desire to comply with school rules. If the student still balks, move to option #3.

Option #3 – Parent Conference and Contract

One or both parents are asked to come to school for a conference with the teacher and principal. At the time of the conference the parents are told the nature of the student's problems and that his misbehavior is unacceptable; in fact, the student will not be able to return to class until an acceptable contract can be drawn up to resolve the situation. The teacher, parent, and student outline the points of the contract and all parties affix their signatures (see sample contract).

Option #4 – Natural Consequences

If it is feasible for the student to make a payment of some type for his improper actions, then this option is used. For example, if a student deliberately breaks a window he pays for it or works it off after school by cleaning around the school grounds. If a student is riding his bicycle contrary to the rules, then the bicycle is to be kept at home for a 30-day period. If a student cuts a class, he is expected to make up the time missed by staying in during noon recesses, etc.

Option #5 – Out-of-School Suspension

Out-of-school suspension may take two forms: (1) immediate suspension, and (2) suspension after forewarning.

1. Immediate suspension:

   When a situation exists that presents dangers to the student or others, immediate suspension can occur, without forewarning. Parents are to be immediately notified and a conference with student, parent, and principal should take place within three days.

2. Suspension after forewarning:

   (Prior to suspension)

   a. The student has the right to know the charges.
   b. The student has the right to offer his explanation of what occurred.
   c. Parents are to be notified in writing and by telephone of the charges against the student.
   d. An appointment with student/parent/administrator should be set on or before the third day.

   (School hearing)

   a. The student has the right to know the charges.
   b. He has the right to offer his explanation of what occurred.
   c. Student and parent have the right to sign a statement waiving the student's right to a further hearing, or
   d. The student and parent have the right to a further hearing.

e. The student has the right to:
   1) A notice of charges
   2) An opportunity to present evidence and witness
   3) Be represented by counsel.
   4) A fair and impartial hearing and decision.

A DIFFERENT KIND OF REFERRAL

One of the greatest boons to good classroom control is for the teacher to take the positive approach. As the Madsen Brothers say, "Catch them being good." By accentuating the positive, behavior problems seem to lessen.

When students do something special or unique at our school, teachers frequently send home a personalized note or a Happy-Gram to share the good word with the parents. When children have done something especially noteworthy, they are often referred to the principal's office. A form for this purpose may look something like this:

COMMENDATION REFERRAL
TO PRINCIPAL

Date:_____

Teacher:_____

Name of Student:_____

Reason for Commendation:

_____

_____

_____

_____

Recommended Action (Please check):

_____ Interview student

_____ Call or send a letter to parents

_____ Make out an award certificate

_____ Other: (Please specify) _____

_____ Announce on intercom

_____ Mention in PTA Newsletter

_____ Call a news reporter

Sample of

SPECIAL CONTRACT

I agree to follow these rules:

1. I will obey teacher's instructions.
2. I will not take other's property.

When I do not follow these rules it is my understanding that I will be sent home* immediately** and will be welcome to try again the next day.

Signatures:

_____	_____
Teacher	Johnny
_____	_____
Principal	Parent

_____

*In the event of working parents the agreement could be changed to say that the student be sent to the office for an in-school suspension or just remain at the office until a parent could come by and pick him up.

**When a student is sent home, the teacher or principal is to call the parents and notify them of the action being taken and remind them that the contract is merely being followed.

REFERRAL TO PRINCIPAL

Name of Student_____

Teacher Making Referral:_____

PROBLEM: (Check applicable item)

_____ 1. Insolence, defiance, or refusal to follow teacher's instructions

_____ 2. Doing physical harm to persons or property

_____ 3. Immoral conduct, or use of alcohol, tobacco or drugs

_____ 4. Cutting class/truancy

STATE SPECIFIC NATURE OF STUDENT'S PROBLEM:

_____

_____

_____

_____

TEACHER RECOMMENDATIONS: (Check applicable item)

_____ 1. Option #1 – Standard Treatment

_____ 2. Option #2 – In-School Suspension

_____ 3. Option #3 – Natural Consequences

_____ 4. Option #4 – Parent Conference and Contract

_____ 5. Option #5 – Suspension

_____ a. Immediate Out-of-School Suspension

_____ b. Suspension after Forewarning

COMMENTS:

_____

_____

_____

DATE: _____

Suggested Reading

Bloom, B.S. 1976. *Human Characteristics and School Learning.* NY: McGraw-Hill.

Charlton, T. & David, K. 1993. *Managing Misbehavior in Schools.* NY: Routledge.

Dreikers, R. & Cassell, P. 1972. *Discipline Without Tears.* 2nd Ed. NY: Hawthorn/Dutton.

Glenn, H.S. & Nelson, J. 1987. *Raising Self-Reliant Children in a Self-Indulgent World.* Rocklin CA: Prima Publishing.

Gordon, T. 1974. *Teacher Effectiveness Training.* NY: P.E. Wyden Publisher.

Kirschner, N.M. & Levin, L. 1975. A direct school intervention program for the aggressive behavior. *Psychology in the Schools.* 12, 202-208.

Kounin, J.S. 1970. *Discipline and Group Management in the Classroom.* NY: Holt, Rinehart and Winston.

Madsen, C.H., Jr. & Madsen, C.K. 1974. *Teaching/ Discipline.* Boston: Allyn and Bacon.

Nelsen, J. 1987. *Positive Discipline.* NY: Ballentine Books.

O'Leary, K.D. & Becker, W.C. 1968. The effects of teacher's reprimands on children's behavior. *Journal of School Psychology.* 7, 8-11.

O'Leary, K.D., Kaufman, K., Kass, R.E., & Drabman, R.

1970. The effects of loud and soft reprimands on the behavior of disruptive students. *Exceptional Children.* 37, 145-155.

Peterson, Q. 1992. *Life in a Crowded Place: Making a Learning Community.* NY: Heinemann Educational Books, Inc.

Wolfgang, C.H. & Glickman, C.D. 1980. *Solving Discipline Problems — Strategies for Classroom Teachers.* Boston, MA: Allyn and Bacon, Inc.

About the Authors

Abel G. Gudmundsen, B.S., M.Ed., E.D.S., has had nineteen years' teaching experience in elementary schools, grades two through six.

Ellen J. Williams, B.A., M.Ed.D., has had twenty years' teaching experience in intermediate grades and is in her sixth year as principal of an elementary school.

Together Mr. Gudmundsen and Ms. Williams have taught classes and workshops in management and control at UCLA, University of Utah, Snow College, and Utah State University. Currently they are conducting workshops in the schools in the Intermountain Area and teaching classes for Utah State University.

Before his death, Rex Lybbert, B.S., M.S., Ph.D., had thirteen years' teaching experience in elementary and secondary schools and was principal of an elementary school for eight years.